You're Never Alone

By

Lon Cole

Lon Cole

A&T Publishing

Puyallup, Washington

You're Never Alone

Copyright 2016 by Lon Cole

All rights reserved under International and Pan-American Copyright Conventions. No Part of this book my be reproduced in any form without written permission from the publisher except by a reviewer who wishes to quote brief passages in connection with review written for broadcast or for inclusion in magazine or newspaper

ISBN 13: 978-1530827572

ISBN 10: 1530827574

Revised April 2016

A&T Publishing

Puyallup, Washington

Alive andThankful.com

Acknowledgements

This collection of poems resulting in this book comes directly out of the support and belief of many who encouraged me through my journey: Number one, I want to express my deepest gratitude to my family. Cris Cole, my wife, she is truly my rock and my life, Alonzo my son and Heidi my daughter, and their families who give me unconditional love. I am inspired by you all every day and your support to share my thoughts and feelings through poetry.

My Thanks to Doug Burgess and John Sharify from King 5 Television, who shared my story with so many, and helped viewers to see Alzheimer's and Dementia through different eyes.

Thanks also for two great friends: Roger Donaldson, who was a great help at the computer, and Dr. John Davis, who was a great support to me at all times.

I'd also like to thank the Alzheimer's Association Bob Le Roy, and Keri Pollock, and so many other friends there. Thank you for asking me to share my verse and tell my story. I enjoy the opportunities to serve as a volunteer partner. Thank you for your support with my journey.

At last, but not least, I want to send a big thank you to my fellow support group members, whom, more than many others, have a deeper , more personal understanding of what I express through my poetry. I am proud to be part of our collective voice.

Thank You

Lon Cole

Introduction

Lon and his own unique experiences has helped him in his poetry. As an artist I have truly admired his talent to express his emotions through his poetry. It is not simple to convey feeling, and he can do it with great ease. His poetry is like a window into his soul that is overshadowed by daily strength that he must demonstrate. I have come to learn as you will after reading this book, that all of us can be taken to the depths of despair. We all can be wounded , but it is within us to rise from it , and become stronger. Word upon word he continues to surprise me, as he so effortlessly portrays the most basic human emotions. From joy and peace to fear and loneliness. His poetry touches on the emotions that unite us all.

Even now, after being diagnosed with the terrible disease of Alzheimer's he has found a way to buoy up those that surround him. After reading this work you will know that you're never alone. His most powerful voice will be the one you will hear as he connects with you through his poetry. Without question, I know that his poetry, his attitude, and simply his presence among those who suffer from this disease, directly or indirectly, are strengthened by him

It is an honor to be his daughter. Life will give to all of us what we need to grow stronger, and he has taught me that our very purpose on this earth is to love our families and our fellowman and to enjoy every minute of this life

Heidi Grace Kress

April 2016

Foreword

Lon's poetry is truly the window to his soul in You're Never Alone, he opens that window for all of us , guides us through heartache to hope, reminds us what we mean to one another and our better selves, and leave us feeling *alive and thankful*

Three of Lon's poems have special meaning for me

"My Partner" is a valentine to a life partner. I shared it with my wife on our wedding anniversary .

Now you're with me always

Wherever I may go

The love that we both honor

Will fill my lonely soul

"Where Am I Going" urges us to hold tight to the gift of life

I'll look for tomorrow and live for today

And hold to the good as it passes my way

I'm strong to the challenge and must be sincere

For life is a gift so precious and dear

"The Vision We Share" Is a life-affirming response to growing old

The visions we share are simple today

That is because we need them that way

You're only as old as your heart wants to be

So live all you can and learn to be free

Lon honors us with his poetry and his service. I'm proud to say that he honors me with his friendship. At the Alzheimer's Association, we offer help and hope. Our vision is a world without Alzheimer's disease. With partners like Lon we are in very good company

Bob Le Roy

President and Chief Executive Officer

Alzheimer's Association

Washington State Chapter

24/7 Helpline 1-800-272-3900

9-11	15
A Brighter Day	16
A Dream Or Two	17
A Family With Love	18
A God Fearing Nation	19
A Great Journey	20
Alive And Thankful	21
Alzheimer's	22
A Medics Call	23
Anger Is A Feeling	25
A Special Gift From Above	26
As We Forget	27
A War Of Hurt	28
A Witness From Above	30
Beauty Surrounds Us	32

Be Brave Be Bold	33
Believe In Yourself	35
Bow Into The Wind	36
Celebrate Survival	37
Challenge	38
Cold As Ice	39
Creation	41
Darkness	42
Darkness Will Follow	44
Death And Beyond	45
Death Or Life	47
Demented	48
Dementia Is Haunting	50
Dignity	53
Discovery	54

Don't Stand Alone	55
Driving For Others	57
Each Step We Take	59
Early Stage	60
Example of Christian love	61
Faith And Beyond	63
Faith A True Course	64
Fear	65
Fitness	66
Forever	67
Forgive And Forget	68
Free From Pain	69
Friends	71
Give Daily Care	72
Goals	73

God Only Knows	74
Good Friday	75
Hard Wooden Floor	76
Having A Shadow	79
He's Now In Heaven	81
He Will Set You Free	82
Hold On	84
Hope Is Near	85
How Can We Show Them	86
I'll Never Regret	88
I Need To Be Free	89
In The Mirror	91
I Served My Country Well	92
It Will All Work Out	94
Late Stage	95

Life A Special Gift	97
Life Gets Tougher	98
Life Is A Journey	100
Live To Be Free	101
Love The Lord	102
Made In The U.S. of A	104
Memories Of Childhood	105
Middle Stage	106
Mother	107
Mother Nature	108
My Partner	109
My Quest Never Ends	111
Nothing To Fear	112
Out Of Sink	114
P.T.S.D	115

Pain	116
Pray To Above	118
Reason For Hope	119
Regrets	121
Remember To Breath	123
Resume' Of The Heart	124
Shadows Of Life	126
She Is My Poetry	128
Show That You Care	130
Show Us The Way	131
Smile	132
So Close To Your Heart	133
Springtime	134
Still Seem's The Same	136
Stress	137

Stretch To The End	139
Summertime	140
Sunday Again	142
The Missionary	143
The Face Of No More	145
The Journey	147
The Moment Is Now	148
The Pain Never Stops	150
There Was A War	151
The Son	153
The Visions We Share	154
The World Is Getting Smaller	155
To Be A Tree	156
Trust in the Lord	157
Truth Will Prevail	159

Volunteers	160
Vote For America	161
Waiting In Line	163
We All Need To Laugh	164
Were On The Same Path	165
What's Real	166
What they Do Is Not Easy	167
Where Am I Going	169
Where Do We Go	170
Winning Is Great	172
Without Any Work	173
With Out A Reward	174
Worried	175
Your Not Alone	176

Nine/ Eleven

Thousands of Americans died that day

It happened so quickly they were taken away

I was at home watching it all

My body was weak, my mind hit a wall

So many people, martyred and slain

We can't let their memories go down in vain

Something snapped inside of me

I need to go back and serve my country

I know I'm to old but what could I have done

I'll pray for our warriors to protect everyone

This dishonoring deed made by those far away

Will be avenged, I pray to hasten the day

A Brighter Day

My day is brighter when you come my way

You lighten my burdens and gladden my day

When you are gone I wander about

When you are with me my heart wants to shout

I may not remember all that you do

But the time that we share carries me though

Please stay by my side as much as you can

Your strength we will share as we walk hand in hand

A Dream Or Two

Everyone has a dream or two
You must be determined for it to come true

When you have found what your looking for
Your quest is not over there is so much more

Give it your all do your best
Pick up your pace, there's no time to rest

You have to work hard to discover your dream
There's so much to do, much more then it seems

Finish your journey then your mission is complete
Remember the taste of victory is always so sweet

A Family With Love

What makes a family be who they are

If they are united their love will go far

Treat each other the best that they can

Give more then you take, learn to understand

Being a father is hard to explain

It's more then the work or the money you gain

A father duty is to protect and provide

Be there when he's needed with arms open wide

A mother is special in so many ways

She nurtures and cares for her children each day

When both work together the family does great

The children are happy and each pulls their weight

A God Fearing Nation

We have always been a God fearing nation

And I hope it's the way that we stay

I fear now that things are changing

That is scary is all I can say

If we lose our faith in America

Then evil can prevail

We can't take our freedom for granted

Or our liberty will suddenly fail

What is left is total anarchy

Each person left on their own

The family will desinergrate

A disaster the worst that we've known

We can not let this happen

We must trust in God above

He will be there to always help us

And surround us with his powerful love

We must fight and stand for our freedom

It is time that we do our part

We must pray for Gods help in the battle

And have hope in all of our hearts

A Great Journey

Dementia is a great journey
Where to many have to go
You can't try to run from it
No matter how much you know
Some say denial is the way
To avoid the pain you endure
Others decide to face it straight on
They hope that there might be a cure
It doesn't matter if your rich or poor
Or have several degrees on the wall
What matters the most is your attitude
Getting up each time that you fall
You can't be afraid of what you might face
The road could feel lonely or cold
Though you are only one of the human race
This is time to be bold
Celebrate survival the best way you can
Remember all the good times you had
So when the dark days come into your path
You won't waste your time feeling sad

Alive and thankful

Some days are good days

Some days are bad

I want to be happy

I want to feel glad

I wish I could remember

Like I used to before

And treasure those moments

That made my heart sing and soar

The names and the faces

I knew everyone

And now there a puzzle

Each memory is gone

I haven't forgotten

How to laugh or to cry
Or say I'm alive and thankful

When someone walks by

Things aren't so bad

They could probably be worse

But I count my blessings

And consider the source

Alzheimer's

Tell me a disease that has no end insight

It can take you in the day or the middle of night

This deadly illness has no cure

It doesn't matter if your rich or poor

It's a modern day plague that must be stopped

Or the toll it takes will go over the top

Those that battle it are few in ranks

But they deserve from us, all of our thanks

It can be conquered, that is for sure

Together we can do it it has been done before

A Medics Call

It's just an old story that I'd like to share
A story of joy and a story of fear
A story told through a young man's eyes
It might make you smile or it might make you cry

Deep in the jungle in the middle of war
There's this 19 year old boy who has been there before
A shout for a medic rings out through the air
The young man gets up and starts to prepare

He knows his duty despite his great fear
To help rescue someone, for all lives are dear
He's shot pretty bad, what should I do
Then another explosion right next to you

The sting of the metal the burning hot pain
Then in come another and stings you again
Your weaker now then you were before
You must do something before there is more

I must help my friend, but what can I do?

Just let out a scream and others will help you

Finally there's someone to take your wounded friend

But sadly they're unable to come out again

Now it's just you, you're all on your own

Bleeding, and in pain, your all alone

You must make a run for it before it's to late

Your chances are slim but there's no time to wait

A dash through the battle bullets everywhere

Just keep running you might make it there

Finally some where to hide so they can't shoot at me

I'm still alive but where could I be

Here come my rescue a small little man

He carries me to safety as he hold my bloody hand

Now I'm safe from all of this war

My friend heads back into the jungle to look for some more

Anger Is A Feeling

Anger is a feeling we must endure

It comes and it goes, this is for sure

Learning to deal the anger we feel

Is a trait we must conquer for anger is real

Some say that anger can do you some good

We must stay in control and not be misunderstood

Learn not to fight every time you are wrong

Say that your sorry, then just move on

Don't let your anger get the best of you

Just swallow your pride and keep your cool

A Special Gift From Above

Be thankful for your blessings
They're a special gift from above
He's only there to help you
To shower your life with his love

A blessing can be eternal
Far greater than you can compare
You're never completely alone my friend
The Lord has so much to share

Each morning you take in a breath of fresh air
The dreams from the night now end
A new day is here for the world to see
The adventure of life starts again

The day is done, you approach night
Did your day go as well as it could
Or was it a day you would like to forget
A day without any good

Blessings come when you need them

Have you learned how to get them to stay

You must count your blessings everyone

Give thanks to the Lord every day

As We Forget

Are we forgotten as we forget

Do we lose all that we are

Or is it a dream that never ends

Just memories so distant and far

We reach, we grab, for a moment in time
It slips by us ever so slow

Some will tell us your losing your mind

The difference we never will know

Where is the truth we actively seek

And search for the answer so clear

It lingers beyond our growing hopes

And relinquishes all of our fears

The answer is near and so plain to see

A puzzle so easy to solve

Just keeping the faith will make us all free

Let God intervene with his love

A War Of Hurt

I starred into the emptiness

To find my way again

My eyes were wondering everywhere

In hope's the curse would end

The feeling of depression

Is hard to push away

It holds you tight in its grip

And haunts you night and day

How do I deal with sadness

That dominates my mind

There's drugs to take and books to read

That helps my brain unwind

I mustn't give into the pain

Or lose the battle within

Just free myself of how I feel

And the war of hurt will end

A Witness From Above

I remember that special day
When Christ was born in a humble way

We sang joyful songs through out the land
To proclaim to the world the Lord is at hand

We watched our Savior learn and grow
Into a man the whole world would know

Far above we heard him speak
Of loving your neighbor and blessing the meek

The sick were healed the cripple could walk
Thousands would follow him to hear him talk

But so quick His mission was nearing its end
And we knew his great suffering would soon begin

We cried as he wept in the garden that night
As the spear pierced his side it was a sorrowful sight

We watched as they laid him in a tomb cold and gray

But three days quickly passed and the stone rolled away

For God showed his glory in a powerful way

The son of God has risen on this Easter day

Our father now reigns with the Lord at his side

Resurrection is a promise to all who will and have died

Beauty Surrounds Us

The children played around the stream

In a land so fresh and green

The mountains stood high and reached for the sky

Their summits could hardly be seen

The trees are tall and rarely fall

The animals run wild and free

The air is clean, sweet and pure

A beauty as far as one can see

This land we love could soon be gone

The peace and quiet we will miss

And in its place a man made world

All void of loveliness

But now the nature surrounds my soul

And follows me where ever I go

How thankful that God made these wonders to see

And dwell within us for all eternity

Be Brave Be Bold

My memory is not as good as before

It's like somebody came by and slammed the door

Sometimes I have fear of what's in store for me

How will I behave and who will I turn out to be

I can't let those feelings take a strong hold

I have to be brave I have to stay bold

We are sent to this earth to learn and grow

To face all our fears and stand up to our foes

We know it won't be easy trying to do what is right

The darkness may come quicker as we lose so much light

But if giving our best is all we can do

Then the battle is not over for me and for you

Remember we are not alone in the struggles that we bare

We have friends and family and God is always there

When we feel low and don't want to go on

It's hope that will carry us and takes us beyond

As we come close to the end of the trail

Remember we were sent here not to fail

Believe In Yourself

Sometimes life appears to be a dead end

You don't have a job, you've lost all your friends

You feel all alone, you have forsaken your church

Something is missing despite your hard search

When you reach the moment when it seems all is gone

That's when you know you just have to push on

Don't give up easy you must hold on to win

You're not alone you're in a place we've all been

It's not over till you give up the fight

You can't quit now when hope is in sight

Things will get brighter as we approach the day

Something will happen so life goes your way

Faith is the answer to all of your plight

Believe in yourself, it will turn out all right

Bow Into The Wind

When your troubles of life begin

Just turn your bow into the wind

Facing your problems is a better way

It will help get you through every day

Life is a challenge for all to bare

Conquer your worries discover your cares

You can't run away from what you feel

Concerns won't leave because they're real

Be strong if you can your not here to lose

Stand up for your freedom it's your right to chose

Don't try to escape from strife you ensue

Because when you do, they will still chase after you

Celebrate Survival

There all kinds of problems that drag us down
But there is always a way to turn them around

We live to be happy, being happy helps us live
But there is no true happiness until you learn how to give

Discouragement is a word that we learn how to fight
The opposite is accomplishment which is doing what's right

So celebrate survival in the best way you can
And honor all of life because living is grand

Be fierce in your battle in doing what's good
Don't waste your time or energy being misunderstood

Be alive and be thankful for all you can be
Count all your blessings, be glad you are free

Challenge

I like a challenge every once in a while
It sharpens my senses and improves on my style

Help me to know what life's all about
To be alive and thankful, I just want to shout

Thinking outside the box is a way to find peace
To build up my strength, and my knowledge will increase

It teaches me lessons beyond what I see
It opens my mind and sets my soul free

Not every challenge will help me succeed
But victories are priceless a triumph indeed

So when a great challenge stumbles my way
I trust in the Lord to hear what I pray

Cold As Ice

The wind is blowing'

The air is cold

It chills my body

Right to my soul

How can I warm

The inside of me

A roaring new fire

Or a pot of hot tea

Though I am freezing

Right to the bone

I'm sure to find

That I'm not on my own

The love from a friend

Can warm me inside

There's no need to fear

And nothing to hide

So though my body

Maybe cold as the ice

The warmth from my heart

Will make everything nice

Creation

Mother nature is our best friend

She always around from the start to the end

All of the animals have their own place

Plant life surrounds us, and fills its own space

Creation is a gift that shines from above

The beauty is amazing as God shows his great love

The earth, sun, and stars have no end

I can see forever, where does it begin?

I witness eternity as I look up in the night

For life continues even beyond my sight

God is the maker of all that we see

He is our creator and set us all free

Darkness

Sometimes life can get very dark

It prays on you, like a man eating shark

Your mind goes blank, it's called a stupor of thought

And when you wake up your brain is all shot

Add a cup of depression and you got yourself in a mess

This happens to me often, I have to confess

Nothing seems clear, your dumbed into a maze

You struggle to exit but everything is a haze

Where is my clarity why am I so lost

I have to do something no matter the cost

Maybe I can meditate and hope I can get out

I am so tied up that I just want to shout

Where is the peace where can I go

There must be a place were calmness will flow

Sometimes my writing helps me endure

The shadows brighten and I feel all so sure

A deep breath or two will show me the way

I'm glad that its over, the night has turned to day

Darkness Will Follow

I'm not afraid to stare into fear

Especially when I'm not on my own

When someone else is by my side

I'm stronger then when I'm alone

I won't remember most of the things

That I was scared of before

That's one of the blessings Alzheimer's brings

There's others that I have to explore

Darkness will follow the years as they pass

I fear I will get that emptiness stare

Void of desire to learn what's new in my life

I suspect that I won't even care

Trophy and awards I used to achieve

Are covered with dust on my wall

My new life is more simpler indeed

The successes I now have must seem small

Death And Beyond

Death comes to us in many ways
In many shapes and forms
Some say death can be very cold
Others say that it's warm

In reality it's a change of address
A time for our soul to be free
The body will rest for a little while
Then soon will unite for eternity

Death's not final but it is all-inclusive
Everyone will experience this event
It takes us in our own due time
An action we can't prevent

But thats okay it's not that bad
Unless we surround it with fear
Though your love one's may seem far away
In truth they are ever so near

No one in their right mind wants to die

They would deny it as long as they can

So when the time comes the Lord is in control

He will be there to take your hand

Together you'll walk through the Vail

The light will be as bright as the sun

You will be encircled by family and friends

You will know and love everyone

You won't be idle during this amazing time

There is so much work to be done

But you won't get tired like you did before

You'll feel great as you bless everyone

Death Or Life

Death is an adventure we all have to face

There is no option for whole human race

Death for so many is something to fear

Especially when death is getting near

Life is a choice we learn to explore

It's what we must do whether rich or poor

Some say that that death has a loud voice

I feel that both are something to rejoice

For life is a gift we all must get through

Death is a beginning of something that's new

Death is not so dark but yes it is real

Life brings you light so you can feel

I'm not in a hurry to meet death at my door

I'll always take life though it maybe hard to endure

Demented

When will it darken

Either day or night

My eyes are wide open

Where is my sight

How can I touch you

If I don't know the way

Why did you leave me

You promised to stay

Who do I hear now

Where do I go

Was I just there

Does anyone know

I have a question

The answers are not there

Does anyone hear me

Are there people who care

The light is still fading

I will loose what is mine

No one to help me

My soul can not shine

Dementia Is Haunting

Dementia is haunting

It moves ever so slow

As it seems to just linger

When you want it to go

It robs you of memory

And erases your thoughts

You often are saying

"I must have forgot"

Life becomes a puzzle

And many pieces are gone

You never will find them

You can never move on

A part of me wants

To get well if I can

Is there someone to help me

As I reach out my hand

I can't be alone

In this journey I make

Could it be just a dream

Or a terrible mistake

I need to be free

I must try to pray

That the Lord will just hear me

And take this nightmare away

I need his mercy

More then ever before

To free me of my suffering

As my heart feels so sore

Then all of a sudden

I know there's nothing to fear

My mind has become clearer

I know the Lord is now near

He has given me loved ones

And friends who will stay

Some day's I may feel lonely

But I know it will be okay

The truth is so clear now

There is hope in the air

My life's in the Lords hands

And I know that he cares

So if you have Dementia

You can just call me

I don't have all the answers

But together, well! We'll see

Dignity

To lose ones dignity is a really big deal

Your losing yourself and all that's real

It's like you've been kick in the back or behind

Or you have been told you're losing your mind

Treat all with respect and dignity too

Someday the finger may be pointed at you

If someone is sick or covered with flaws

Don't make it worse no matter the cause

Give them a smile and a warm hand shake

Look eye to eye and a friend you will make

Discovery

Anger was my focus

When answers were not there

What I wanted was solutions

And to be with those who care

I was buried in my fear

Not understanding why

Though you saw me smiling

My heart would often cry

I showed a different side

Of what I wished to be

A soul that's trapped from inside out

That truly longs to be free

Then the answer came to me

In such a simple way

To live your life the best you can

And celebrate each day

Don't Stand Alone

Share the burden we carry

Lift the weight off our souls

Help us find the humble way

To conquer the troubles we know

Worries can be a heavy weight

Loading you down with pain

Find a way to free yourself

There is so much we can gain

Don't stand alone in the work you do

Remember who is by your side

The Lord will always be there for you

With his arms open wide

You won't fail in your mission

To free you from so much strife

The Lord is here to save you

He'll be there through out your life

You need to hold your ground

Especially when you feel low

Be there for those who love you

Your faith will make you whole

Driving With Others

To drive a car equals independence
The choice to go where you can
Along comes responsibility and liability
That can be hard to understand

What do you do when it's no longer safe
To drive your car anywhere
How hard it must be to hang up your keys
To show other drivers you care

Some say it's safe to drive just a little
As long as it's a familiar place
How do you decide how little is to far
Not everyone has the same case

If you are driving because you can't let it go
Think hard before you decide
Are you doing whats best for others
Or is it just a matter of pride

Choose wisely my friend as you set in the car

Which side you will sit on today

Will you be cautious and safe for others

Or let reason be thrown away

Each Step We Take

Traveling down the lonely road

May seem like no one cares

When someone helps you carry the load

The trip is light to bare

Each step we take if on our own

The journey appears undone

There is no need to cry or moan

Together you are more then one

Do not fret if another is near

To lend you a helping hand

Be thankful for the one so dear

Who will truly understand

Where ever you go or where ever you've been

Our Lord is always there

To help you have the strength within

Your burdens he will share

Early Stage

There's a middle aged man just standing around

He looks confused and little bit down

He just came from a store, and is straining to see

He's wondering where his car might be

He has a bad memory when he has to recall

And struggles with crowds especially in the mall

It's hard to accept that he no longer drives

That he has to depend so much on his wife

He tries to do the best that he can

To give all that he meets a helping hand

Example Of Christian Love

One day I looked out the window

A surprise was waiting for me

My neighbor was working in my yard

How blessed could a man ever be

It was an example of Christian love

That we all should try to pursue

He taught me a lesson I needed to learn
That the Lord would always do

He gave all he could to his fellow man

Including his life so free

That we might learn to live like him

And do good to all we might see

My neighbor is really a good example

Of how a Christian should act

I know if the Lord did ask him

He would give the shirt off his back

Where can we go or ever could do

To show our love for the Lord

We could live like he would want us to

And learn to worship to his accord

Faith And Beyond

Faith is the anchor for the soul

It follows us wherever we go

Losing a love one is an awful plight

But when faith comes along things turn out all right

God has a way of steering you straight

He mends what you've lost, and carries your weight

Things aren't always the same, I guess thats okay

For God is in control, and will show us the way

The ones that we love who are gone from our sight

Some day will return to brings us new light

Faith A True Course

Faith is such a special word

It rings with strength and peace

And gives to each one of us

A hope that will not cease

Sometimes life seems all so dark

The road is marred with haze

It passes by us ever so quick

And leave us in a daze

But faith makes our path crystal clear

Our journey is straight and true

It opens the doors that are usually closed

And the old and forgotten become new

Believing is a way of life

No one can mar the course

For truth will prevail and always win

When the Lord becomes our source

Fear

Fear is a feeling we all have to face

Don't run from your fears you won't win the race

Everyone get scared quite often we know

The fear that we feel may come and go

It's what we do when the fears in our way

Do we face it straight on or do we let it stay

There is something good when we face all our fears

Developing a strength that endures through the years

When you are scared and fear starts to flow

Just stand up straight and let your fears go

Fitness

Being healthy is the right thing to do

It lengthens your lifespan a decade or two

Staying healthy is a lot of work

Don't take it lightly but don't go berserk

Exercise often and eat the right foods

Be a positive thinker maintain the right mood

Don't throw in the towel when your feeling low

That is the time when you can't let go

Strive to be fit work at it each day

It will all be worth it you must not delay

Always remember take care of your health

The value is priceless far greater then wealth

Forever

When your pulling down the shade of life
Try not to suffer from worry or strife

Those that you love are not far away
The ones who passed on get closer each day

They seem to be saying in a soft tender voice
That where you end up is a matter of choice

The life that you live is hard to foresee
Each step that you take will help make you be free

Be wise in your living whatever you do
And make life an adventure until it is through

You wont be forgotten there's so much to see
Your eyes will be open to all of eternity

Forgive and Forget

To forgive and forget is so hard to do
The pain that you bare can stick close to you
Where does one go when it's time to forgive?
Who's there to help you how do you live?
God will not leave you He's right by your side
So cough up your guilt and swallow your pride
If you can learn to forgive you can learn to forget
It may not be easy but it's always worth it
Forgiving yourself that's not and easy road
Just give it a try it will lighten your load
You have to remember your not on your own
The Lord will be with you so you're never alone
So get on your knees and start to pray
Try to make it a habit each and every day
I know that he listens to each humble prayer
He will forgive and forget and show that he cares

Free From Pain

Abuse is a word we all learn to hate

It's sting can leave your soul in an awful state

All that hurt may make you want to hide

It steals your respect and erodes all your pride

How can we move on and deal with the pain

The scars can be real and so can the shame

The memories are strong though your mind wants to be free

You can close your eyes tight but still you can see

Who can help you what can they do

Let God have your pain he will take it from you

Pray to be free have faith that you can

The Lord has suffered all he truly understands

With Gods help your mind can become clean

You may become weak but on God you can lean

The past can be gone, the good future is near

No longer the pain no longer the fear

Oh what a blessing to finally be free

Now you can follow your true destiny

Friends

True friends our here to stay

They give much more then they take away

They know how to listen when you need them to

Their words are wise, and usually true

They won't leave you when the chips are down

When the road is rocky they will still be around

Real close friendships will last for a life

You're lucky if they are your husband or wife

If you lose a friend the pain is deep and long

When you gain friend you feel happy and strong

A friendship is a two way street

To be a friend makes the circle complete

Give Daily Care

It must be a challenge to give daily care
Day after day you must always be there
When you get tired how do you rest
You have to have someone who will give it there best
Caregivers are a special breed
They care and love you and see to your needs
Caring for someone close in your life
Most often it will be a husband or wife
Time is your foe each trial you must face
You have to keep going till you finish the race
And if you fall down you must stand up again
A day will arrive when it comes to the end
It may be a sad day a day of great pain
But you gave it your best with nothing to gain
The one that you served may have moved on
But the love that you shared will never be gone

Goals

I truly wonder about setting new goals

There always the same and don't come from the soul

Lose lots of weight and exercise more

Pick up the mess that's spread on the floor

Goal after goal when will it stop

It's driving me crazy my brain wants to pop

Maybe a few goals I'll chose at this time

I've got to do something I losing my mind

I guess I'll just change the date on the goals from before

That's plenty of goals I don't need anymore

God Only Knows

When life is lost there's a special cost
Where money can never go
Each person gone still lives on
Inside of another's soul

The pain is real and can't heal
No matter what someone does
They strain there eyes and often cry
When their thinking of who it was

Remember this you'll always miss
The memory of one you loved
But in your mind you can find
Gods peace that comes from above

So were we go God only knows
It's strictly a matter of choice
The closer we get we have to admit
Its time for us to rejoice

Good Friday

Many say Good Friday was a sad day for sure
It was all so painful for our Savior to endure

He hung on the cross and experienced such pain
And gave his life freely but it was not in vain

It's hard to imagine the agony he bore
As the nails pierced his wrist, and so much more

He cried to his father to forgive those below
To grant them all mercy, only love he could show

When he was brought down he was cold and pale
Then came a horrible storm with lightning and hail

He was carried away to a lonely grave
I could never be that loving or ever that brave

Three days later the Lord did rise
As witnessed by angels a wonder to their eyes

A Hard Wooden Floor

Once I went to the old country store
I wasn't doing much my life was a bore

I met an old man I had never seen before
He was dancing the jig on the hard wooden floor

I asked him his name as he continued to dance
He starred right at me as if in a trance

I asked him again as I let out a yelp
I looked at the others who offered no help

And finally he spoke just one single word
He answered "why" how strange and absurd

I had enough from this coy little guy
I hollered so loud I let out a cry

What is your name I wont ask you again

He calmly answered me back "why" as he continued to grin

Thats all I could take, I had now had enough
Now he will see that I can be tough

I hit him right square then I hit him once more
But I swear he was still grinning as he fell to the floor

Now it was just him and I on that hard wooden floor
Until a little old lady walked through the door

She looked at me with pain in her eyes
And let out a scream "why o why"

What could I say I just lost my cool
The answer was senseless I felt like a fool

Then the old man stood up and still had his grin
But I had given him a bloody nose and cut on his chin

She came over to comfort him and started to cry

Again she cried out "why o Why"

A that moment I realized what I had done

I beat up an old man that was just having fun

What is his name, I asked as she carried him by

His name is Wyatt but we just call him Wi

I am not having fun my life still a bore

As I'm setting in jail on a hard wooden floor

Having a Shadow

Sometimes life is like having a shadow
That follows every step that you take
At first it seems like a honor
In time all you want is a break

You need your own space a place all alone
But your shadow denies what you seek
It wears you down and tires your soul
Your spirit becomes also weak

It's time to realize why your shadow is near
To remind you of darkness and fears
The burden you bare is a lesson to learn
The light you give erases their tears

So now you suffer and worry
Because your shadow is always near
But when their alone how sad they must feel

Their life becomes hollow and filled with fear

What can you do to brighten their day
Is there a way you can share
Give them the love they truly need
Then they will know that you care

He's Now In Heaven

I miss my Dad he's been gone for a while

He always knew how to make me smile

On Friday we would often play cards

He was always willing to help in the yard

He said he was lonely since Mom was gone

His house was so quiet except when the TV was left on

He often spoke loud because he couldn't hear

He was blind in one eye but he never showed fear

He fought in two wars a sailor was he

When I got my medal he was so proud of me

He's now in heaven with Mom at his side

Just waiting for the rest of us with arms open wide

He Will Set You Free

Dementia is a very serious disorder

It attacks the brain and has no borders

Your memory leaves and nothing remains

All that is left is a dying brain

It just isn't fair how it picks who will die

If your wealthy or smart it won't pass you by

The older you get the higher the chance

What can you do now you must take a stance

Where ever you go what ever you do

Trust in the Lord he will be there for you

You can get through this you can put up a fight

Laying down and giving up just isn't right

Keep the door open do all that you can

Life is worth living you just need a plan

Plan for the future be all you can be

Show faith in the Lord and he'll set you free

Hold On

If your the one who the gives the care

Your challenge is strong and may seem unfair

You must endure what comes your way

And hold your ground as their slipping away

Be there to listen as long as it takes

Be able to give though your heart wants to break

Cherish the time with those that you love

Hold to the memories and pray to above

Be strong if you can life will go on

Don't lose your hope when your love one is gone

Hope Is Near

Don't give in whatever you do

Hope will always be there for you

If your challenges seem hard to bare

Remember that the Lord always will care

Hope can be a way of life

It battles the anger, and conquers the strife

So when you are struggling you need not to fear

For where there is hope the Lord will be near

Believe and trust in all that is true

You won't be alone no matter what you do

Give hope a chance, it never will fail

And hold your ground for good will prevail

How Can We Show Them

There is a group of women and men
Who are called to give their all
Though their husband and wives are often gone
It's the family that answer the call

How can we serve and help them
To make their burdens seem light
What can we do to show them
That the service they give is right

Many of our military have families
That have to survive on their own
While husbands and wives are on missions
The families must stay home alone

Think of our warriors in battle
And pray that they all will return
Always remember their sacrifice and service
Our love and respect they have earned

We must never forget the families

There must be something we can do

To lift and show them are greatest praise

For God would expect it from you

Reach out to show that you care

Just give them a helping hand

Your soul will feel better deep down inside

There's always a way that you can

I'll Never Regret

I'll never regret the day we first met

I hope that you feel the same

Your the only one that I truly loved

I'm glad you carry my name

We were very young and leaned on each other

To get through the troublesome days

Two individuals traveling the same path

A path held together in so many ways

We are getting a little bit older now

And wiser in our advancing years

So when things get tougher on us

We are not swallowed up by our fears

Stay by my side as long as you can

How quickly the future passes by

Together there is nothing we can't do

As long as we give it a try

I Need To Be Free

Your traveling on a peculiar trail
Each step you take something new is unveiled

Then you come up against a great wall
The first thing you notice, is the wall is to tall

You look to the left and then to the right
It keeps on going far out of sight

How will you get on the other side?
That is a puzzle you must confide

If only the wall had a way to get through
You could continue your trek and all that is new

Suddenly you discover a transparent door
How strange that you had never seen it before

The trail keeps on moving on and on
Far past the door, the wall and beyond

The path still get better beyond what you see

But the door is locked and you don't have the key

Then you realize what's in store for you

You can no longer move forward no matter what you do

You call out to the Lord "I need to be free"

Please help me God I must find the key

Then the door opens all on its own

Your eyes stop crying and your heart ceases to moan

The trail is now clear for you to move on

Now all your worries and troubles are gone

You have discovered what eternity truly can be

Its never ending, you will for ever be free

In the Mirror

I looked in the mirror, I stared so deep

Who is that person who's started to weep

Do I know him is he a friend

He seems to be troubled, and alone again

Will he be lonely the rest of his life

Does he have someone maybe a wife

I wonder why I can't remember his name

He looks so familiar I'm going insane

Someday I'll ask him why he just stares

He is so stoic and doesn't seem to care

Well I have to go now is all I can say

Maybe I see you some other day

I served my country well

I served my country well

I did my time in hell

I fought the battle we all did loose

Without the drugs without the booze

Why did we die why did we bleed

Was it for power or was it for greed

And now our country wants to forget

The sacrifice of the Viet Nam vet

Someday war will come again

What could we tell our sons

What honor could we promise them

When they see what we have done

How sad and lonely they will feel

As they march off to war

With stories of the older vets

Who fought in vain before

So now I tell America

From me and all my friends

Who gave their arms, legs and lives

So freedom would never end

It Will All Work Out

Our lives are filled with troubles

Sometimes they're hard to bare

We can't always do it on our own

Some burdens we just have to share

A wise woman has told me

That "It will all work out"

It may be hard to accept that

We tend to always have doubt

You have to develop strong faith

Before your journey is done

Know that God won't forsake you

That's why he sent his Son

No one said it would be easy

I don't think it was meant to be

Life can be hard in so many ways

But it's worth it to you and me

The path that we follow may be rocky

But we have to go all of the way

We are never alone as we travel

And there's all kinds of ways we can pray

When we pray we must listen

To the Lord's powerful but still small voice

And when we receive his council

It's still always a matter of choice

If you don't pray hard or choose wisely

You are still saved by his great love and grace

Remember someday you will meet him

As he holds you in his loving embrace

Late Stage

I hear a voice call out to me

A weak little sound is all it can be

Trapped inside an old tin can

Is what is left of a once young man

Where does he go when he can't find the way

He's covered in darkness on a bright sunny day

Now he is quiet he can no longer talk

He rides in his chair forgot how to walk

He hears very little and can't reply

A little bit of life still twinkles in his eye

He stares into emptiness he can hardly see

But someday that old man will finally be free

Life Is A Special Gift

Life is such a special gift

That brings us joy and peace

But sometimes things aren't so good

That's when pain and suffering increase

It's how we really live our life

That determines which way we sail

Doing our best is the final test

A test we must never fail

Surviving all the storms of life

Must be are truest quest

The effort that we all put forth

Has to always be are best

Be not afraid but face your fears

For God will help you win

The victories that you have in life

Truly has no end

Life Gets Tougher

Life gets tougher everyday

It seems like a puzzle that is hard to play

No matter how much or how we complain

We lose much more then we ever could gain

Its like a big battle that will never end

And all of the troubles come again and again

Our goals they seem hollow and beyond what we know

The paths they get longer and move ever so slow

Is there an answer a way we can win

Or is it a huge circle that has no end

I must believe a solution is there

And surround my self with all those who care

No matter how complex my troubles may be

here's always another who will be there for me

I know there is help where ever I go

I hold to the steady and blessings will show

One by one the good will prevail

No matter what happens I know I wont fail

I count every blessing so precious they shine

I learn to be thankful and open my mind

Life Is A Journey

I want to lift everyone that I can

To look to the future and think life is grand

To rid help themselves of the pain of before

To find the strength that can help them feel sure

Sure of the hope of a bright sunny day

That good will happen as you move on your way

Life is a journey we all must endure

And hope we can live a life that is pure

Enjoy the gift that a good life can bring

Always give thanks to the Lord our great king

When life comes to an end you can say with great pride

I tried to live my life on the right side

Live To Be Free

In our country we live to be free

To be whatever we want to be

We're taught to be the best that we can

That we are unique whether woman or man

If we work hard there is nothing we can't do

Discovering our dreams is what we pursue

It doesn't matter if were strong or meek

What matters the most is the truth that we seek

The knowledge we find may be our reward

We should always remember it came from the Lord

Can we get on are knees to say thank you?

Believing in God is the a good thing to do

Love the Lord

Did You live the life the Lord gave you?

Are you now on the real course?

Have you wasted the precious time you have?

Do you recognize the true source?

You must pass the test you were given

If you want to go to the head of the class

You won't be graded by how many you failed

Or even how many you passed

What determines your score of today

Is the effort that you put in

To show how you honor the Lord

As you triumph over your sins

Don't get discouraged or low

Just do all that you can do

The Lord intercedes in so many ways

He's there to help get through

So discover the life that he gave you

A brilliant life it will be

Learn to love the Lord in every way

You will learn how to make yourself free

Made In The U.S. of A

Where is America where has it been?

Is it the same country we use to live in?

What's made in America is always the best

American made will pass every test

Somethings have turn up side down

When you look for the best it's never around

Where can we go what can we do

Every thing is made cheaper for me and for you

What do we stand for where do we go

Is made in China the best we can show

We better wake up before it's to late

For our children's sake we really can't wait

We must get back to made in the U.S. of A

Or our rights and freedoms can be taken away

Memories Of Childhood

Children like to play and have lots of fun
They laugh and they giggle in the brightly lit sun

They like to discover things that are new
They're usually honest and talk straight to you

Alone they get nervous that's how it should be
Together with others they jump and run free

My memories of childhood were the best times of all
We could play all day with one little ball

Then when it was time to go inside
Mom would be waiting with her arms open wide

We were all very lucky we didn't need much
With hamburger helper mom had the magic touch

Now that I'm older life is so complex
You don't talk to each other now you just text

Middle Stage

Trapped in between the darkness and light

Is a little old man alone in the night

He doesn't remember like he used to before

Trying to talk becomes a great chore

He walks very little there's no where to go

When asked if he'll join us he always says no

He wears the same clothes it's so hard to change

When he's in a crowd he feels very strange

There's not much more I could say about him

Except the light in his soul is beginning to dim

Mother

Mother is a special word

Her loving touch a glow

She can warm the heart and sooth the pain

As she helps her children learn and grow

Mother is a righteous word

A gift from God is she

To teach and show the art of love

And to unite the family

Mother is an important word

Her mission here on earth

To bring to life every being

Through the miracle of birth

Mother is a joyous word

We must honor and revere

For where a caring mother stands

We know our Lord is near

Mother Nature

I looked into the sky one day

To see what mother nature had to say

Look at my greens look at my blues

Such pretty colors I offer you

Be still my friend don't say a word

And you will hear the chirp of a new born bird

All of this beauty is my wonderful gift

To open your eyes and give you spirit a lift

For I am hear to help you feel free

You can soak in the sweetness as far as you see

My Partner

I can still remember

As far back as can be

The memories that I treasure

Are the ones of you and me

We loved and laughed together

Each moment was a gift

A precious treasure aways

That gave my heart a lift

Yesterdays are fading

Before today appears

When I seek the answers

I find my recent fears

All I know is nothing

Now its all so still

Are you there to help me

My empty mind to fill

You are there to show me

I must take your hand

Time is quickly passing

Will I understand

Now your with me always

Where ever I may go

The love that we both honor

Will fill my lonely soul

My Quest Never Ends

I search for the answer My quest never ends

And hope to be valiant in the battle I must win

I will call for my champions to conquer all my fears

And I'll triumph with valor as my time nears

I will look past the darkness and kneel as I pray

I must look for the question as I ponder it each day

And when I'm convinced, that truth will prevail

I will give thanks to God for us he'll never fail

Nothing To Fear

Climb aboard, the trip is free

Don't be afraid of what you might see

Open your eyes as wide as you can

Try to remember and to understand

Where are we going? I'd like to know

Somewhere new I really hope so

You count the people who are coming along

I'll be the tour guide and sing them a song

Song of discovery, a new tune I hear

We're just having fun there's nothing to fear

When do we get there? I really hope soon

Its getting darker I don't see the moon

My eyes are wide open there's such a bright light

I feel so at peace it all seems so right

So many people I know everyone

I can't believe it's as bright as the sun

They are all smiling and looking at me

I've got to go further there so much to see

I feel so at home in this wonderful place

I since God is near I can feel his grace

I think this is heaven I hope that it is

There's no pain or sorrow only pure happiness

Thank you for coming with me my good man

It makes me so happy to be together again

Out Of Sink

Sometimes the heart isn't in tune with the brain
Confusion and heartbreak is all that remains

Where do you start to make the repairs
Both are essential they both need good care

Neither can function all on it's own
They both would fail if left alone

The spirit is the glue stick that helps them unite
When there working together everything is right

The mind needs its peace the heart needs its calm
If they team up together they create a strong bond

So remember when the mind and heart are out of sink
You'll forget how to feel and be unable to think

P.T.S.D.

Fear rocks my soul every night

I can't let things be I'm wound up so tight

The thoughts inside my mind are weirder then me

They scare me a lot and won't let me be

The pills that I take subdues all my harm

I'm luckier then most I won't cause alarm

I go every week and their I just talk

But sometimes I need to go for a walk

I'm haunted by warriors that won't let me go

They call out to me and reach deep in my soul

The dreams are the worst I have to say

I'd sleep much better if the dreams went away

It puzzles my brain is there any hope for me

All I can hope is that someday I'll be free

Pain

Pain is a feeling that can last for a lifetime

It seems like it will never go away

It's there to remind us of how the body works

There could be a pain for every day

There's all types of pain we all know well

A pain to the body and a pain to the soul

Our pains can be treated with all kinds of pills

But the pain to the soul is hard to let go

Sometimes we abuse the pain pills we take

That can create heavy pain to the mind

It's like a big whirlwind that spends around and around

Or like a large spring trying to unwind

But the pain in your soul goes ever so deep

And stings you from the inside out

It will make you depressed as you long for relief'

it erupts in loud angry shouts

You find yourself pleading for help

From friends and those you love

You even drop to your knees with a humble request

And you seek guidance from God above

There's know way to know exactly how pain will fall'

But it's easy to know that it will

So trust in the Lord who took on all of your pain

He'll be there for you as you take on your hill

Pray To Above

Prayer is a way to speak to the Divine

Its a chance to share whats in your heart and mind

When you pray to the Lord, you show that you care

You hope for the answer and have faith it is there

Praying is not a one way road

We must carefully listen in a spiritual mode

The answers may not be what we want them to be

They will be right and they will set us free

How long and when should we pray?

Have a prayer in your heart every moment of the day

You don't have to pray for others to see

Pray can be in secret and on your knees

Reason To Hope

Do you have a reason to hope?
Or is it beyond what you can bare ?
Are you staring into the darkness?
Do you feel like no one really cares?

Go back to having hope again
It will help you conquer your pains
With out it you are probably lost
The faith in yourself can't be sustained

Hope equals faith in so many ways
It gives you a chance to survive
Your put on the front steps of God
It helps you feel that your alive

Don't lose your hope keep it close by
You'll need it when times get bad
Hold yourself steady lean on the Lord
Especially when your feeling sad

Believe in yourself you won't be let down

You didn't come to the earth to fail

No body said it would be easy for you

But hope will always help you prevail

Regrets

When you have regrets

Your living in the past

Life becomes a do over

Because your dye is cast

So many times in life

I regret the things I've done

How hard it's to say your sorry

To every single one

Give me a second chance

To correct the mistakes I've made

File them past my mind and heart

In one long single parade

If I could make the corrections

That would ultimately change my course

I could be free of all the pain of regret

That's followed by so much remorse

So give me some new hope

To make what was wrong a right

Resolutions is what I seek

Put the misery out of my sight

I must not forget

To repent of all my sins

So if I am forgiven

I can never do it again

Remember To Breath

Remember to breath it's a wonderful gift

Inhale Gods love he will give you a lift

There is so much beauty in this world we know

Most comes from nature as it surrounds our souls

The pure white snow makes you want to shout

And the crystal pure water brings you joy no doubt

The colors are so vivid when the sun starts to shine

Mother nature has a beauty that can blow your mind

The greatest of wonders is pure magic to see

When we enter nature our spirits are free

As I take it all in it's so hard to believe

I have to remember it's my time to breath

Resume' Of The Heart

I am still here ,where else could I be

Life is a struggle, but its worth it to me

Some days are dark ,and others bring light

Sometimes I feel awkward, some days I'm just right

One thing I know life is a gift

It gives us meaning and my heart a big lift

I may not be the same as I used to be

Memories fail, but you can always trust in me

I may be a little rusty in somethings I know

But I can learn quick ,and I never work slow

Sometimes I'm wrong I'm the first to admit

I wont make excuses I'll just get right to it

If I forget to show up one day

Don't send me packing, I want to stay

Believe in me as I do in you

Together there is nothing we can't do

Shadows Of Life

The shadows of life are usually dark
Trouble and worries appear
You search for the way to erase the thoughts
While the memories grow into fears

Sometimes it feels that it's all a bad dream
You'll wake up and just feel fine
While your awake you'll search for the answers
That are locked up deep in your mind

Finding the key that unlocks the brain
Is as hard as the key to your heart
When both are open a mystery is solved
Then believing will begin to start

There lies the hope your soul can now feel
No matter how dark it had been
Now your prepared for whatever comes
With peace you find from with in

Joy is the conqueror of all that was lost

The victory so sweet and pure

Free from the shadows that linger so long

Your spirit and body can endure

She Is My Poetry

I've been a poet for many years now

My poems have had many themes

The poems that touch my heart the most

Is when I write of the women of my dreams

A wise man once said to me "She is my poetry"

So true were those words to my soul

Together we have traveled for many years

And bring deep love and respect wherever we go

All of the gifts she has brought to me

Like the children we hold so dear

I'm in awe how she always stands by me

When she has seen all my weakness and fear

My love for her will last forever

I pray that she feels the same

When I meet the Lord face to face

I know that I will call out her name

I believe that life is more then chance

Only God can determine our fate

When one falls in love it can be a blessing

Together we will opens heavens gate

Show That You Care

See the glow on your face, and the smile in your eyes

Show the world who you are and why you are wise

When you laugh from your soul there is much you can share

So never be afraid to show that you care

The kindness you have carries joy in your hands

Your wisdom bows to all it commands

The work that you do equals the service you give

You teach us all how to share and a better way to live

Your absence of fear is a sign of your courage

Your easy to trust and you don't get discouraged

But the most of all is to feel all of Gods love

That happens to be his gift from above

Show Us The Way

Where can we go when the road looks dark

What do we do or say

Will we be lost in deep black night

Will anyone show us the way

Sometimes life get to hard to bare

We search for the answers unclear

When we find all that we seek'

We will face it with courage not fear

Is our journey a lonely road

Will we find help from the light

It glows on the path to show us the way

It helps us to know if were right

The shadows we see may limit our hope

We'll gather our course and follow the Lord

For without him we're lost in despair

Smile

The gift of a smile can brighten our day

It raises us upward, and colors the gray

A smile is the sunshine each person can show

It warms all our spirits, and gives light to the soul

It requires some work when your sporting a frown

To create a smile is much harder then it sounds

A smile will always bring you new life

It's a way to repeal all worries and strife

When you live with a smile you can truly take pride

For all those that see you will be happier inside

So close to your heart

Those that we love are so close to our heart

We cling to their memories as they slowly depart

We want to do something that will keep them close by

While looking for comfort we want to know why

Why are they leaving when we want them to stay

How can we help them while they are drifting away

Hold to the good times and know how you feel

Each moment is precious and ever so real

Keep living your life the best way you know

And hold to the rod and never let go

As your day arrives and it is your time to leave

They will honor your memory and always believe

Springtime

This is a special time of the year
Things change right before your eyes
The colors become so vivid
The clouds open up from the skies

The sun it shines more often
And the cool air starts to warm
The animals become more active
And the mountains change there form

Spring has so much to offer you
The streams are crystal clear
The melting snow feeds all of life
And brings nature also near

The grass it looks much greener
The trees they sway so free
You can hear the sounds of everything
From a waterfall to a buzzing bee

The smell of spring is amazing

There's so many smells to enjoy

Just take a deep breath and soak it all in

There's no need for you to be coy

Be thankful for what we're given

And the special time of spring

So if we listen carefully

We can hear mother nature sing

Still Seems The Same

Grandchildren are a blessing for us all

They come in all sizes from large to very small

They help your day go very fast

The energy they generate will give you a blast

There easy to spoil they brighten the day

And when they're gone you miss them right away

They make you feel younger though they can wear you out

They never stop moving as they move all about

When it is time to say goodbye

The hardest thing is to watch them cry

When they get older they still seem the same

They move a little slower but live up to their name

Life would be boring if they weren't around

That's why I look forward to hearing their sound

Stress

Some day's you feel like your ready to blow
Your so anxious you can't even think
Your all tied up in one big knot
And your spirit is beginning to sink

Some call it anxiety others say it's stress
when your wound up so tight
Your body starts to shake all over
Your heart is ponding and nothing is right

Why does the body react in this way?
There must be some pill you can take
Is it a feeling or physical pain
You feel like your body will break

Your feeling so tense you just want to shout
You pray that it will not stay
Your hurting so much you want to cry
You'll do anything if it just goes away

Your down on your knees asking for help

You figure there's no where else to go

You've taken the pills you listened and talked

And finally your heart starts to slow

The nightmare is over at least for tonight

The sun shines brightly and clear

The battle subsides it was a good fight

Your soul is filled with good cheer

Stretch To The End

We can't win every battle we fight
Losing happens sometimes in our life
It is what we do when we lose
How we deal with the pain and the strife

There's a part of me that says just go on
Have the faith it will all work out
The other part wants to push me down
Then I get angry and just start to shout

I must endure and not lose my dream
I must realize its within my reach
If I just hang on a little bit longer
I will gain the wisdom that I seek

Don't throw in the towel or call it quits
When you are within reach of your goal
Hold to the rod and stretch to the end
Have faith in your self and your soul

Summertime

When summer comes it's a great time for all

We all get so tired of winter and fall

Spring is a warm up for summer that's sure

The snow melted water is crystal and pure

The nights become shorter the days can get hot

The grass needs more water and you mow it a lot

Some say summer is a time to have fun

We all seem happy as we enjoy the warm sun

It's when we vacation and there's so much to do

There's places to go that are exciting and new

Summer brings adventure and memories to last

Though the time that we share can pass by so fast

So quickly it happens and summer is gone

The coldness returns and it's time to move on

Fall, winter, and spring, and summer can be

A time to find joy a time to feel free

Nature is a wonder a blessing we all can share

A precious gift from God above that we must treat with tender care

Sunday Again

Yes it is Sunday again

And to church we all will go

For it's been a very long and hard week

And theres so much to learn and know

Yes it is Sunday again

And eagerly awaits the Lord

For us to enter into his house

And pray and worship to his accord

Yes it is Sunday again

He fills our hearts as we sing

To honor our Lord Jesus Christ

Who is creator redeemer and king

Yes it is Sunday again

And the meeting has come to close

We will climb in our cars and head for our homes

With the spirit of the Lord in our souls

The Missionary

I met a man a while ago
Whose spirit seemed to shine and glow
The words he spoke reached deep inside
Far past my fear, doubt and pride

I've learned so much since the day we spoke
Of truth, wisdom faith, and hope
I've made commitments to serve and obey
To forsake all my sins to study and pray

The water was warm as I rose from the font
A joy filled my heart what more could I want
The gift of the Holy Spirit came upon me
My eyes were opened my soul was now free

Life's still a great challenge a battle I must fight
But now I have the knowledge that I chose the right
If I follow the Lord as long as I live
I will walk in his presence my sins he'll forgive

Now those I meet and those who I know

All seem to say that I shine and glow

I share my sweet secret in hopes they will see

That they can have joy and make themselves free

The Face Of No More

We all have seen faces

That we've seen before

But it's hard to forget

The face of no more

Why did he go

He should have stayed

Where is he now

As I'm drifting away

I don't feel I'm grounded

I'm covered in pain

And haunted in sadness

While his memory remains

I must find the answers

To where he has gone

And open my soul up

So I can move on

We are never alone

His spirit is now free

I must keep on living

For him and for me

Some day I'll see him

And remember his face

Then we will share

In a brothers embrace

The Journey

I took a look deep down inside

Far past my guilt, worries, and pride

The deeper I went the more painful it was

Will I get past the pain and discover it's cause

I continued my journey exploring my thoughts

Way past the battles my mind often fought

I might understand whats bothering me

If I just go deeper I'll set myself free

Then it just happened like opening a door

So fast I was moving much deeper then before

My mind had gone the deepest it had ever been

The suffering was over the pain was starting to end

My spirit was free how clear I could see

A glimpse of the heavens was open to me

The sweetness of peace filled my soul

This was my quest this made me whole

The Moment is Now

The moment is now

The future is near

I can not forget

And I must try not to fear

What ever I see

Where ever I go

Life seems so fast

Why can't it be slow?

Things just pass by

I reach but there gone

I would like them to stop

But they always move on

A thought or a memory

Confused every day

Where are the answers?

Will I find the way?

I must not forget

That memories are for not

There is more to my life

Then what I forgot

The Pain Never Stops

Pain is a feeling we all have to bare
Theres all kind of pain its hard to compare

When I'm hurting deep down inside
Thats the worst kind of pain I must confide

It seems like for ever the pain never stops
Your hurting so much that your heart wants to drop

Your left on your own confused and depressed
You call out for help but your mind is so stressed

Physical pain you can't often recall
Emotional pain makes your skin want to crawl

The best way to deal with pain that I feel
Is to share it with God as I bend down to kneel

He helps us be free from all kinds of pain
It rest on his shoulders as peace we obtain

There Was A War

If in this land

There was a war

And my son fought

Hard and was slain

Along with grief

I would share some pride

To know that he died

Not in vain

But he died in land

So far far away

From all that I loved

And once knew

And the Lord

I do say will

Hear what I pray

And will let my poor son

Come though

It matters not

Where ere he may be

Or how he

Was taken away

His time in my life

Was such a great gift

A treasure a memory

That will stay

The Son

The Father, The son, and The Holy Ghost
Are the supreme being of us all
Adam and Eve were the start of the human race
They were the very first humans to fall

The Sons mission was to redeem all mankind
To free us all from a spiritual doom
He sacrificed himself and took on our sins
Three days later he rose from the tomb

He guides, and counsel us with his love
No greater love there ever could be
If we obey him and hold to the course
We will live with our Lord and be free

His life was an example of how we should live
The lessons he taught were so pure
If we could follow the path that he led
Will make it to heaven for sure.

The Visions We Share

To be young again is a dream come true

We learn as we age that life isn't new

When we were young we could really go

Now that we age it all seems so slow

We get tired easier than we did before

We were always in a hurry and lived to explore

Now time is so precious we pay a high price

We dream of the days when all was so nice

The visions we share are simple today

That's because we need them that way

Your only as old as your heart wants to be

So live all you can and learn to be free

The World Is Getting Smaller

It's such a crazy world out there
People mixed up and don't seem to care

Their actions are unusual I have to say
Some should be committed and carried away

Others could be quite normal it is hard to tell
Lost in a darkness they aren't doing very well

Wanting for answers confused by the replies
Not understanding and still asking why

How can you reach them are they all lost
We must try to help no matter the cost

Everyone feels a little crazy now and then
Failing to help them is truly a sin

The world is getting smaller it's different each day
The changes are gigantic in every way

To Be A Tree

The mighty tree it stands so tall

As a lonely man I look so small

I hope and pray that I could be

So tall and strong and sway so free

But I am just a lonely man

Who walks along the lonely sand

And dreams of mountains and skies so blue

with giant forest and clear lakes so cool

He sees no war this giant green

No auto wrecks or man made machines

Dear God I dream and pray I will see

When all mankind is like my friend the tree

Trust In The Lord

The challenges of mortality never cease
You face them every day of your life
We live to find each day of peace
We're surrounded by worries and strife

We call on the Lord to rescue us
From problems we seem to find
We search for the answers to bring us peace
And to ease our troubled minds

The love of the Lord fills our soul
With a calmness we often seek
Temptations may soar beyond are control
And trap us when we become weak

Faith is the answer that sets us free
Believing when we need to know
Delight in our God will help us be
Able to achieve all our goals

We'll become stronger when we trust in the Lord

The mind and heart will unite

Our prayers will be answered to his accord

And the wrongs maybe conquered by right

Truth Will Prevail

Believe all you can that truth will prevail

For no matter what happens your not here to fail

Your life is so precious beyond what you know

And when your confused its hard to let go

Try not to be selfish learn how to share

For Gods special gift will always be there

Help others to find their way

Always remember to pray every day

Pray in the morning pray every night

The answers you get will always be right

God hears all the prayers that come from the heart

Trust me, it's never to late to start

Volunteers

Volunteers are a noble career

There givers that serve us ever so dear

Without them not much would ever get done

They work for the many and give to the one

Where would we be without them today

There service is worthy in every way

They have a great gift they are willing to share

You become a better person whenever their near

So reach out and give without a reward

The time is well spent and you'll never get bored

Vote For America

The constitution is inspired word
Made to last for all of time
Anyone who tries to tear it down
Is committing a treacherous crime

So many have fought and died
To keep our country free
We have to make America great again
It must be all it can be

We are one nation under God
And will always stand for the right
Though our country may be in decline
It's time for us to unite

I'm proud to be an American
I have had my time in war
I've watched the young bleed and die
All patriots and so much more

How do we honor the strong and brave

And make it all worth while

It's time to vote for America

And go the extra mile

Waiting In Line

Waiting in line can be such a pain
While others move forward I still remain

How long will it take I'll be here all day
It's driving me crazy how long must I stay?

Please call my number before I go mad
Why is everyone starring at me? Do I look that bad?

I can't even remember why I got in the line
If I don't get out of here, I will lose my mind

Somebody cut thats not fair to the rest
I'm tired and I am angry at the whole stinking mess

"Closed for Lunch" whats happening to me
I think I am losing it what else can it be?

I'm out of here I can't wait anymore
I will come back tomorrow but its such a great bore

We All Need To Laugh

It's good to make fun of yourself now and then

For telling a good joke is never a sin

We all need to laugh as often as we can

It clears your mind and helps you understand

The physics of laughter is an interesting site

It's good for your body both day and night

Laughing will help when in pain or depressed

It erases the worries and gives your body a rest

So let out a laugh and see what it can do

I'm sure you'll feel better and not have the blues

Were On The Same Path

When your disabled you struggle each day
To try to live your life in a normal way

Those who can't walk,hear, or see
Are still the same as you and me

We live on the same planet and breath the same air
We're not asking for more we just want you to be fair

If we try to help and give all that we can
It makes it easier to live in this land

Were on the same path to a better life
Together will conquer our worries or strife

What's Real

Giving care is not an easy task

Especially for those unaware

Quite often your feelings are kind of masked

In and effort to show that you care

Each moment of time spent on others behalf

Brings peace to your troubled soul

It opens your heart where your feelings are trapped

So emotions and love can flow

A tear or a smile they both mean the same

An effort to show how you feel

This giving of oneself is more then a game

In serving you will discover what's real

So reach out to others

Just give it a try

It may seem somewhat scary

But I promise you won't die

What They Do Is Not Easy

I sit and watch some really great warriors
Who walk by me each day
They are the best this country has
They are working to serve the USA

What they do is not an easy job
They deserve our greatest respect
They do it because they love their country
So we can keep the peace in check

What can we say or do to help them
How can we show that we care
We can treat them descant and with honor
And always keep them in our prayers

I hope when you get a chance you'll thank them
Just give them a break when you can
If they weren't there to protect us
Then evil would take over our land

They wear an uniform most of the time

You may see them with their families at their side

We need to do our best to help them all

And keep our arms open wide

Where am I going

Where am I going will I ever get there

Will somebody know me does this all seem fair

I'm sure there is someone who feels what I feel

But has trouble expressing the pain that is real

But I must keeping going and steer from the past

For each day is hopeful, and nothing is cast

I'll look for tomorrow and live for today

And hold to the good as it passes my way

I'm strong to the challenge and must be sincere

For life is a gift so precious and dear

Where Do We Go

Sometimes our memories come and go

They pass through are mind fast and slow

We try to hold them as tight as we can

We end up confused and don't understand

Where did they go? Why are they gone?

Will they come back? Or have they moved on?

Most memories we lose are short term I' m told

It usually happens when we start getting old

"I can't remember" is a familiar phrase

Our minds end up in a dark misty maze

It's happening more often I'm afraid to say

We seem to forget something every day

Where do we go to get help that we need

Someone that's wiser then me I concede

Whoever we find must really care

They must earn my trust and be willing to share

Winning is great

Winning is great when your on the winning side

Doing your best brings you true pride

Victories are measured by the work you put in

Each time you fall down just get up again

Effort is equal to energy spent

I'll tell you secret , I'll give you a hint

You must give all you got then give a little more

You'll feel the triumph and your spirits will soar

A champion is someone who never quits

They keep on running when they want to sit

Treat everyone as equals don't act like the best

Prove that your great by acing the test

Be a good sport in all that you do

Shake hands with everyone when the contest is through

Without Any Work

When your without work you have little pride

You feel so desperate you wish you could hide

A person needs work to move them along

Without a job things turn out wrong

If they are willing to give all effort they can

Then give them a chance they will work hand and hand

There's people who really want a career

They will study and learn and go anywhere

There not here to joke make fun or play

They just want to work hard every day

Without A Reward

Giving is an act of love

That the Lord would always do

When we give without reward

Our blessings are never through

Where, when or how we give

Is not as important as why

In giving all that we can in life

It's worth more than money can buy

Everyone needs to help in some way

In doing so our spirits will climb

Helping others who can't help themselves

Is a wise way to spend money, talents and time.

You should honor your service

By being as generous as you can

Whatever you give is worth more than you have

There is joy in giving others a helping hand

Worried

When you are worried you can never let go
Your haunted, your scared and it bothers your soul

You cry out to everyone as you wipe away the tears
It drives you crazy and loads you down with fears

Your covered with questions the answers you seek
Can somebody help you your mind's getting weak

Clear answers would help in so many ways
Worries can linger and go on for days

Where is the clarity you desperately need
We must solve the troubles we have to succeed

Will give it a try as much as we could
If we can get help it will do us some good

When the worry is over you feel great relief
Now you can say goodbye to sorrow and grief

You're Never Alone

I have been told that you're never alone
I wish it was always that way
So often it seems you're all on your own
They leave when you want them to stay

You search for the right answers
But even the questions are gone
You rest for a moment or two
But all your worries still move on

The quest it seems so shallow
As the victory is slipping away
Solutions they are too hollow
There is darkness even at day

I am not afraid to face it
I must do the best that I can
And if I fall short in my journey
I will get up and start again

Made in the USA
San Bernardino, CA
03 June 2016